Successful Consultancy

in a week

JOHN WILSON

Hodder & Stoughton

A MEMBER OF THE HODDER HEADLINE GROUP

Orders: please contact Bookpoint Ltd, 39 Milton Park, Abingdon, Oxon OX14 4TD.
Telephone: (44) 01235 400414, Fax: (44) 01235 400454. Lines are open from 9.00 -
6.00, Monday to Saturday, with a 24 hour message answering service.
Email address: orders@bookpoint.co.uk

British Library Cataloguing in Publication Data
A catalogue record for this title is available from The British Library

ISBN 0 340 73781 6

First published 1999
Impression number   10 9 8 7 6 5 4 3 2 1
Year   2004 2003 2002 2001 2000 1999

Typeset by Multiplex Techniques Ltd, St Mary Cray, Kent.
Printed in Great Britain for Hodder & Stoughton Educational, a division of
Hodder Headline Plc, 338 Euston Road, London NW1 3BH by Cox & Wyman Ltd,
Reading, Berkshire.

**the Institute
of Management**

F O U N D A T I O N

The mission of the Institute of Management (IM) is to promote the art and science of management.

The Institute embraces all levels of management from student to chief executive and supports its own Foundation which provides a unique portfolio of services for all managers, enabling them to develop skills and achieve management excellence.

For information on the various levels and benefits of membership, please contact:

Department HS
Institute of Management
Cottingham Road
Corby
Northants NN17 1TT
Tel: 01536 204222
Fax: 01536 201651

This series is commissioned by the Institute of Management Foundation.

C O N T E N T S

Most managers dream of becoming independent consultants. Free spirits that drift from one grateful organisation to the next and earn enormous fees. Such images of a consultant's life are sadly just illusions, but the reality is still exciting and the job satisfaction can be extremely high.

Consultants are not a special breed. Any manager with the right experience can establish a successful consulting business. All that he or she needs are a few extra skills and the courage to 'go it alone'.

The practical steps that follow cover the professional, financial and business management skills a would-be consultant should possess.

Sunday	What are consultants?
Monday	What sort of consultant would you like to be?
Tuesday	Setting up shop
Wednesday	Getting started
Thursday	Money
Friday	Promoting and marketing
Saturday	Winning new business

What are consultants?

The meaning we now give to the word consultant, 'a person whose business it is to provide professional advice', is quite modern. It dates from the last quarter of the nineteenth century when it was first used in the major professions like medicine and engineering. Today, the title, 'consultant', can apply to anyone, from a person giving a multi-national corporation board-level guidance to someone proffering advice on cosmetics in a department store.

Despite its wide and general application, the commonest use of the title consultant is to describe those who provide professional advice and assistance to businesses and other types of organisation. It is with these people, the *management consultants*, that this book is concerned.

What do consultants do?

There is no shortage of definitions of management consultancy, but one of the best is that given by the Institute of Management Consultancy (IMC):

A management consultant is an independent and qualified person who provides a professional service to business, public and other undertakings, by

- identifying and investigating problems concerned with strategy, policy, markets, organisation, procedures and methods
- formulating recommendations for appropriate action by factual investigation and analysis with due regard to broader management and business implications
- discussing and agreeing with the client the most appropriate course of action
- providing assistance where required by the client to implement the recommendation

Like any all-embracing summary of a complex subject, the IMC definition is rather lengthy and ponderous. However, it contains a number of key words which, if looked at separately, tell us a lot about the detail and focus of what consultants do. The words are:

- *Independent* – being free from vested interest and able to take a detached view of an organisation's strengths and weaknesses
- *Qualified* – whether by experience, education or some other means, a consultant should be qualified to conduct an assignment

- *Identifying* – consultants must possess the perceptive and analytical skills needed to enable them to identify and isolate problems
- *Investigating* – helped by their independent status and mandate to probe, consultants are usually better able to investigate problems than are internal inquirers
- *Recommending* – the outcome of most consulting assignments is the presentation of recommendations which reflect the investigation findings and the consultant's knowledge and expertise
- *Implement* – most consulting assignments now go beyond the provision of reports and recommendations: they involve the consultant in the implementation of these recommendations
- *Action* – increasingly, consultants are being asked to take a more proactive role by working with the client's management team; sometimes for periods of months or even years

Specialist or generalist?

Whilst there are some generalist consultants, the vast majority specialise in one of the main management functions. There are also sector specialists: consultants who work in just one industry or type of organisation. These narrow specialists are now becoming less common as more and more companies feel they can learn from the practices in other industries and actively seek consultants with cross-sector experience. Unfortunately, such enlightenment is taking time to reach all parts of the public sector. Most local authorities, hospitals, police forces and the like are conservative in their selection of management consultants.

They usually favour only those with extensive experience in their particular area of public service.

Functional specialists
The majority of consultants specialise in one of the four main areas of business activity: *finance, operations, marketing* and *human resource management.*

- *Finance* – this is a highly specialised area in which only the most experienced and highly qualified consultants can find work. The function makes significant use of consultants, but they are mainly from specialist consulting groups, often associated with large accountancy firms.
- *Operations* – this is a rich area for the small consultant. As well as considerable opportunity in mainstream manufacturing, there is a steady demand for help with distribution, storage, quality management and other production-related activities.

- *Marketing* – whilst the specialist marketing, selling and public-relations help needed by medium-sized and large organisations can only be supplied by big consulting firms, with special facilities and back-up services, there is plenty of scope for independent consultants able to meet the less demanding needs of smaller organisations.
- *Human resources* – this function offers the greatest scope for the smaller consultant. HR departments are usually kept as small as possible, leaving many of them short of resources and skills. Training and development are the prime areas for consulting activity, but HR managers often seek help with things like selection, appraisal and administration.

Cross-functional specialists

Consulting opportunities are not restricted to the four major functions. There are several management and technical disciplines with applications in more than one functional area. Some, like IT, health and safety and communication skills, apply to virtually every function. Work in these disciplines is particularly exciting and rewarding; it is also a growth area for consultancy.

The ideal cross-functional consultant is someone who can combine a thorough knowledge of his or her subject, with a broad understanding of the main management functions. Such people are always in demand.

Consultant types

Today's successful management consultants fall roughly
into three categories:

1 *Problem-solvers* – consultants who provide expert help
   in identifying, investigating and solving clients' problems;
2 *Helpers* – consultants who are called in to help with
   tasks that the client's management could well do
   themselves but, for a variety of reasons, are seeking
   outside help;
3 *Collaborators* – consultants who are able to integrate with
   the client's management team; working alongside them to
   provide advice and guidance but also taking a 'hands-on'
   role in designing and implementing projects. Such
   assignments, which are often concerned with
   organisational change or the introduction of new methods,
   provide a growing source of work for small consultants
   and one that many are finding highly rewarding.

Do clients prefer big consulting firms?

The idea that large consulting firms always have the edge
on small firms or consultants working alone is a complete
myth. There are, of course, many assignments that need
the multi-disciplined teams and technical back-up that only
large consulting firms and specialist institutions can supply.
Equally, there are plenty of smaller, straightforward
assignments on offer that large firms cannot or will not take
on. There are also clients who are not keen to approach
large firms with small assignments. They fear that the
work will be given to an unskilled trainee or else farmed
out to a part-time associate.

Large firms are afraid of small ones

A senior executive from a large consulting company, when speaking about competition, said that he was not too concerned about the risk of losing business to other large firms. 'These we understand,' he said. 'We know how they operate and how to outmanoeuvre them. What we fear are the small firms and independent consultants. They appear from nowhere, take the assignment and disappear again without trace.'

Those wishing to set up as independent consultants have little, therefore, to fear from the large firms. Their only serious competition is from people like themselves.

What skills do consultants need?

The skills of a successful consultant fall into two distinct categories:

1 *expert knowledge* – experience and knowledge in a chosen area of expertise;
2 *consulting competence* – the ability to conduct a range of assignments, identify and solve problems, assist and influence clients, deliver good advice, produce well-written reports and deliver convincing presentations.

A checklist of consulting competences

The ability to:

- listen
- probe
- analyse
- communicate
- interpret and report
- identify problems
- provide solutions
- persuade and convince
- plan and implement action
- act fairly and impartially
- be always honest and professional

What do consultants get wrong?

Consultants are easy and popular targets for criticism. They claim to be experts; a condition that invites attack. However, amidst all the unfair criticism are many genuine complaints about the things some consultants get wrong. It is important to note these criticisms.

The most common criticisms are:

- overcharging clients
- delivering poor-quality service
- wasting time at the client's expense
- being insensitive to the client's corporate culture
- behaving in an arrogant and superior way
- spouting jargon

- writing incomprehensible reports
- communicating badly and infrequently
- not producing what their proposal promised

This list of criticisms should be carefully studied by anyone thinking of becoming a management consultant. Avoiding all of these sins will not guarantee success, but committing one or two of them will certainly guarantee failure.

Why do organisations use consultants?

Organisations seek help from consultants for one of two basic reasons:

1 They need the specialist advice and practical assistance that is readily available from consultants but difficult to obtain from any other source.
2 They require a range of services that may be available from several sources, but consultants are usually the most cost-effective suppliers.

When do organisations seek help?

Organisations seek help from consultants when they are faced with needs that fit into one or more of the following categories.

Consultants are called in when an organisation is:

- *in need of special input* – new systems, methods, techniques or procedures are required but the organisation lacks the knowledge, skill and experience needed to introduce them
- *facing a crisis* – the organisation has an operational, marketing, financial, HR or some other business problem that it cannot resolve using internal resources
- *looking for an objective opinion* – the organisation needs the opinion of an experienced, knowledgeable, independent observer who will not be influenced by internal politics or personal prejudice
- *about to enter a period of change* – at times of change, an organisation's management team may come up against a range of new problems, and needs the help and guidance of someone who 'has been there before'
- *feeling the need to improve its practices* – the organisation is looking for new ideas and ways of improving existing systems and procedures
- *looking for some short-term help* – the organisation needs some experienced hands about the place but is not prepared to hire additional staff for what may be a temporary workload
- *in need of training and development* – the organisation has staff-development needs but lacks the skilled staff to organise the training, coaching and mentoring required

How do organisations select a suitable consultant?

The classic 'textbook' view of how organisations select consultants is that they choose those who can:

- demonstrate professional skill

- show an understanding of the client's problem

- prove they have expertise in the assignment topic

These three factors appear regularly in research findings and surveys, and whilst the priority order may vary, there are not many people who do not accept that when choosing a consultant from a number of bidders, most clients will opt for one whose professional qualities they admire, who shows understanding of their needs and who can demonstrate relevant knowledge and experience. This does not mean that other factors like cost, original ideas, previous client experience etc. are not important; but it does mean they are less important.

Whilst most consultants claim to understand these selection criteria and their relative importance, one would hardly think they do from the way they behave and market their services. Many still feel they will improve their chances of being selected if they 'look the part', and try to do this by producing glossy brochures and operating from opulent premises. Others try to convince people their services represent the very latest ideas and thinking. Yet another group places great importance on pricing, and bombards potential clients with 'evidence' showing that when it comes to 'value for money' they outstrip all their rivals.

All good stuff; but it does not represent the key things clients are seeking.

> When clients make their final choice, it would seem that the personal qualities and experience of the consultant outweigh most other factors.

Summary

Today, we have defined different types of consultant, looked at their basic required skills, and discussed why and how organisations seek their services.

What sort of consultant would you like to be?

Today, we will look at some of the basic decisions that must be made before setting up a consultancy, and at the skills a person needs in order to be successful.

- Where to specialise?
- What experience have you got that will sell?
- What extra skills are needed?

There is plenty of scope

We cannot talk about consulting as if it were a neatly defined profession in which broadly similar people do more or less the same things in much the same way. Nothing could be further from the truth. The range of skills that consultants display, the many thousands of specialist areas in which they work and the seemingly limitless variety of approaches they have to meeting clients' needs, make consultancy one of the most richly varied areas of professional activity.

The scope offered by all this variety is one of consultancy's greatest attractions, but for the person entering the business for the first time it raises some daunting questions. Questions like, 'What sort of a consultant do I want to be?', 'What shall I specialise in?' and 'What new skills will I need?'

For a small number of people, these questions pose few problems. This fortunate group is made up of those who already have a lot of knowledge and experience in some specialist subject that is in constant demand by an established market.

However, for the vast majority of would-be consultants, the situation is not so straightforward, and some important choices have to be made before they can get started. These choices are about the areas in which to specialise, the level at which to operate and the type of consultancy service they would like to provide.

Where to specialise?

Most people follow their instincts and go for the things they most like doing. Not necessarily a bad choice, but it involves two dangers:

1 Is your favourite interest something the market requires and clients will pay for?
2 Are you good at it? (We are not always at our best when doing the things we enjoy most.)

If the answer to both questions is an unequivocal yes, then the search *might* be over, but if there is the smallest doubt, an objective assessment of your skills and competences is called for and the next section should be read very carefully.

What have I got to offer?

The best way to identify your real strengths is to analyse each of the skills and competences about which you feel confident. To do this, you might find it useful to prepare a three-column checklist.

In the first column, list the things you are good at; in the second column, note down a few career events that show your success at applying these skills; and in the third column, make some comments on how marketable each item might be.

Take time over this exercise and be completely honest and objective about what you write in each column; especially the third one.

General skills are important
When making this analysis, there is a tendency to concentrate on technical skills and on experience in which product or systems knowledge was the dominant factor. However, make sure also to include examples of success in applying general skills – like communication, negotiation, training, counselling, presentation and administration. These general or ancillary skills have a dual significance; they might form the basis of some marketable consultancy

service, but more importantly, they are essential skills in the
business of being a consultant.

What have I got that would sell?
Having completed an analysis of the things you are good at,
the next stage is to identify those that might be developed
into a service you could sell. Again, the secret is to be as
objective as possible about the things you select; and ruthless
in rejecting anything about which there is any doubt.

Begin by making a list of the key skills identified in the
earlier exercise, and against each write a brief description of
the service you feel you could provide. Alongside each of
these proposed services, write an outline strategy for
selling it. This strategy should contain:

- the form in which the service would be offered –
  advisory, training, hands-on involvement, etc.
- the market – list the sectors and potential clients
  within them
- means of access to the market – how this market
  can be reached (contacts, networking, trade
  organisations etc.)
- any special features you can offer

Making a final choice
With any luck, the above exercises will have narrowed
down the choice of specialist areas to a manageable
number. It does not have to be *one* specialist area. Indeed,
there are dangers in working in a single highly specialised
field where a sudden downturn in demand can put a
consultant out of business. Equally, it is important not to
claim expertise in too many subjects. Most organisations

are suspicious of anyone who looks like a Jack-of-all-trades. Only the gurus like Peter Drucker and Tom Peters can claim to be experts at everything and be believed.

Consulting can be hard work

There are many reasons why consulting work takes up more time and effort than most people anticipate, but two are more significant than the rest:

1 *Marketing* – the time involved in finding clients and winning contracts can be much greater than most people imagine (see Friday and Saturday).
2 *Lack of support* – being self-employed means that for most of the time you are alone, without direct support, and all those jobs that other people did for you when you were working in an organisation, like typing, filing, making appointments, buying supplies, office administration and making the coffee, you now do yourself.

There will be disappointments
Selling consultancy requires a stout heart. Sending out 100 letters and getting no replies; spending four days preparing a proposal to which the prospective client does not even respond; and driving 200 miles in mid-winter for a 20-minute meeting with a group of people who do not know what they want (but decide you cannot supply it); can all be rather disheartening. Learning to accept these disappointments, and living with a low return for one's marketing efforts, are essential stages in developing the attitude needed to cope with the less glamorous aspects of being a consultant.

> The good news is that the buzz one gets when winning a contract or completing a successful assignment makes up for all the earlier disappointments.

Family support

Most consultants begin by working from home; and many continue successfully to do so on a permanent basis. Homeworking is looked at in more detail tomorrow, and at this stage it is sufficient to say that the full support and encouragement of one's family are essential if this arrangement is to work.

Consulting involves running a business

- Never lose sight of the fact that a consultancy is a business.

- Like all businesses, consultancy is about buying and selling. A consultant sells services – always striving to get the best possible deal from the customer – and buys materials and resources – seeking the best value for money from the suppliers.
- A consultancy, like any other business, grows for one reason: it provides goods and services that customers find more satisfactory than those of other competing suppliers.

> A consulting business will succeed if it provides a service that exactly meets the client's needs, at a quality that exceeds the client's expectation, delivered in a way that shows a genuine desire to provide customer service and at a price that is seen to be fair.

What practical skills will I need?

Yesterday, we listed the competences consultants need to complement their expert knowledge and make them into rounded professionals. This list is long, but many items are largely covered by three key areas of communication skill:

1 listening
2 writing
3 presentation.

Listening
Listening is not the same thing as hearing. Hearing is a straightforward physical ability; listening is a complex

activity concerned with what we *do* with the things we hear. Failure to grasp this difference is why few people make a conscious effort to develop their listening skills. The idea of formal training in listening would seem ludicrous to most people, yet it is the primary stage in the receipt of all forms of spoken communication. It is said that misunderstanding accounts for more than three-quarters of all spoken communication problems. Many would argue that a failure to listen properly is the prime cause of this misunderstanding.

Listening is an *active process*; and it has to be worked on. The good listener always prepares for a meeting or interview by:

- thinking about all the subjects that are likely to be raised
- listing the key issues about which clear information will be needed
- making a note of all the questions to which answers are expected

At the meeting or interview, the good listener:

- sits where the speaker can be seen and heard clearly
- makes notes, and summarises the stages reached in a discussion or presentation
- takes care to hear what the speaker is actually saying and not what he or she expected or would like to hear
- notes the speaker's body language
- ignores distractions and does not allow the speaker's appearance, presentation style or choice of language to take away attention from what is being said
- questions the speaker until he or she is absolutely clear about what has been said

- where possible, provides a summary feedback to the speaker on all the key points, to confirm understanding.

Following these guidelines, and listening with attention, interest and courtesy, is often described as 'active listening'. Given the large amounts of information he or she has to absorb, often with limited opportunity for a second hearing, active listening is a skill that no consultant can afford to be without.

> Much of a consultant's information-gathering takes place in the context of an interview, defining interview in the broadest sense. This makes it essential for a consultant who is unfamiliar with interviewing skills and techniques to seek out appropriate training and advice.

Writing

Most consulting work involves a considerable amount of writing. Proposals are usually required in order to secure work, detailed reports are the normal culmination of assignments, and in between there is the preparation of a wide range of notes, summaries, manuals, training material and other written documents. All this makes the ability to write well, quickly and succinctly an essential requirement of every consultant.

It is important to get a clear idea of what sort of writing we are talking about. Consultants are not expected to produce works of literature. Colourful phrasing and clever wordsmanship are not what the client expects or deserves. The writing qualities that clients appreciate above all others are:

- *brevity* – managers are usually busy people and often regard time spent reading as non-productive. Try to keep reports and papers short, to the point and free from padding and repetition.
- *clarity* – this means being understood by *everyone* who is likely to read the material, which may include people whose intellectual, technical and managerial skills range over a wide spectrum.

Writing style

The ground rules of good business writing are as follows:

- Choose simple words and avoid polysyllabics wherever possible
- Steer clear of jargon, and always use the most general word that adequately describes your point
- Keep sentences short and sharply focussed by restricting them to only one point or statement
- Paragraphs should be as short as the subject will allow, but do not divide long paragraphs just to look neat and orderly – the break between paragraphs should feel natural
- Layout is nearly as important as content and can be a great aid to clarity and impact
- Whilst taking care not to create too much clutter, make full use of subheadings, bullet points, boxes and diagrams to simplify the text and give emphasis to key points

These rules have been tried and tested over many years, and the wise consultant will follow them diligently.

Presentation

The ability to make a good presentation, be it to a handful of people or to an organisation's annual conference, is an essential part of the consultant's skill repertoire.

There is a range of occasions when a consultant will be asked to make a presentation, but the most common are:

- *marketing presentations* – when competing for a contract or simply putting a new idea to an existing client, a consultant will usually be asked to make a formal presentation;
- *presenting results* – most consulting projects end with the presentation of recommendations or findings. This can be anything from a modest event, involving a small group of people, to a whole series of presentations to different groups that take in almost the whole workforce.

Stages in preparing and making a presentation
The following steps apply to most situations and should be
carefully followed when making a presentation or helping
others to do so:

1 Set clearly defined objectives.
2 Gather material (facts, data, visuals etc.).
3 Structure the presentation.
4 Select the visual aids and presentation techniques to
   be used.
5 Prepare speaker's notes.
6 Reconnoitre the venue if possible and rehearse the
   presentation there, or in a place that resembles it.
7 Anticipate questions and prepare answers.

Learning from and making full use of experience

> For many clients, the 'product' they are buying when
> they hire a consultant is experience.

For a consultant just starting out, the experience he or she
has to offer will be that gained from previous employment,
from out-of-work activity and from life itself. Making use
of this experience is not simply a matter of remembering
what happened. More detail will be needed than most of
us can store in our memories, and it is essential that a
consultant brings together in some formal way all the
information available about relevant experience. This will
mean digging out old reports and papers, checking the
reference material found helpful at the time, noting where
material not readily to hand can be accessed (and that it is
still there) and marshalling all this into a filing system that
is simple and quick to use.

Ongoing experience
Once in business as a consultant, there will be new and
highly relevant experience in plenty. Make sure this is
carefully recorded and referenced for future use. Do not
rely solely on papers prepared for the clients. A good
consultant will keep notes on the way an assignment has
progressed, the problems encountered, people's reaction to
recommendations and suggestions and much more. It is
these notes that will be of greatest value when facing a
similar situation in the future.

Mistakes provide valuable experience
Mistakes are an important part of a consultant's experience.
Do not try to hide and forget them; record them, analyse
them and *learn* from them.

Project management
Managing a consulting assignment, be it one involving a
single consultant for a few days or a whole team for several
months, is an exercise in project management, and the
consultant must understand and apply a wide range of
project-management skills.

> A good knowledge of project management is a useful
> tool in the consultant's kit.

Keeping up to date
The final 'skill' we will look at today is that of keeping up
to date. This may be less of a problem at first when a
consultant comes straight from full-time employment
where it was comparatively easy to keep abreast of new
developments when surrounded by colleagues who
collectively monitored information and happily shared

their findings. As a solitary consultant, keeping in touch is less easy but actually more important because consultants are expected to be up to date in their specialist subjects and always ahead of their clients.

Staying well informed, when running a one-person business, requires positive action. Subscribe to the appropriate journals and read them. If not already a member of the relevant professional body, join and make full use of its information services. Most professional bodies have reference libraries and information departments; some even have advisors who can be consulted on difficult issues.

Do not forget public libraries. The main libraries in towns and cities offer a wide range of services including on-line access to national and international databases. Most have special business sections which are a mine of information and practical help.

Local and regional agencies like Tec, Chambers of Commerce and Business Clubs are another valuable source of information; especially on matters concerned with the business side of running a consultancy.

Summary

Today we have looked at choosing an area of specialisation, offered some advice on lifestyle, commitment and business requirements, and discussed further practical skills needed.

Setting up shop

Today we are looking at some of the practical aspects of
setting up a consultancy. These include:

- premises – where will you work?
- secretarial help
- equipment
- stationery and documents

We will also look at the preparation of reports and
proposals, a basic business plan and some of the things that
affect the client's image of a consultant.

Where shall I work?

There is a strong temptation for many people to rush into
acquiring premises from which to work. For some, this
desire comes from a belief that clients will not take

seriously a consultant who does not have a 'proper office'. This is a complete myth. Clients hire consultants for what they do; where they do it is immaterial. Buying or renting premises is also an expensive undertaking, and the idea of starting a business with a substantial overhead cost does not seem wise.

Thanks to modern technology, working from home has never been easier, and unless it presents insurmountable problems, the 'home-office' should be the way to start.

Working from home
Ideally, the home-office will be a separate room used for no other purpose. However, if such a luxury is not possible, take courage: many successful consultancies are run from the corners of bedrooms, landings, loft conversions or even garden sheds.

The whole process of working from home is made easier by the availability of cleverly designed furniture and equipment that allows the 'office' to be cleared away when the working day is over and the room returned to its original use.

Whilst the practical arrangements for a home-office may present few problems, the presence of someone working at home all day can disrupt family life. A well-lit landing or the space under the stairs that nobody knew what to do with might be the ideal location from a practical point of view, but if this means confining the children to the kitchen all day and establishing rules like 'no vacuuming before 6 p.m.', then the less comfortable but secluded corner of the guest bedroom may be the better choice.

Office premises

If, for whatever reason, working from home is not an option, there are often alternatives available that are less expensive than renting a conventional office.

Local small businesses may have spare accommodation which they will hire out at rates well below those charged by office landlords. Such an arrangement can sometimes have added benefits, like a receptionist/telephonist service and access to photocopying and other office services. In most towns, and some rural areas, there are 'enterprise programmes' that help small businesses get started by providing office space and basic services at subsidised rates.

Secretarial help

As with premises, some people are tempted to hire secretarial help from the outset, but in most cases this would be unwise. Employing staff is a complicated, time-consuming and expensive business; and for the newly established consultancy it is rarely necessary. Personal computers enable most people to operate without direct secretarial support, and there are agencies around to lend a hand when things get busy.

Modern computers are easy to handle, and once keyboard skills are mastered, the advantage of being able to work directly into a personal computer (PC) is invaluable – even when secretarial help *is* available. The growing use of e-mail and the Internet is another reason why consultants must be able to use a keyboard and be reasonably computer literate.

Equipment

Having decided where the office will be, and accepted that for the time being you will be secretarially self-sufficient, the next question is what equipment will be needed.

Personal computer
Obviously, a PC is an essential requirement, and the choice of model will depend largely on the nature of the work the consultant undertakes. For most people, a basic machine with good word-processing and graphic capability is all that is needed. Beware the slick salesman who will try to sell you a more powerful machine than you need, along with a mass of expensive business software.

Furniture
Apart from a good desk, and some storage arrangements for files and papers, there is no need for elaborate office furniture. One exception is a chair: consultants spend long hours at their desks, and backache is a common ailment. A decent chair is not a luxury, it is a health aid.

Fax
A fax machine, or the capacity to send and receive fax messages on a PC, is essential. Most fax machines also serve as rudimentary photocopiers.

Photocopier
High-quality photocopying machines are expensive, and the workload has to be high to justify the cost of hiring or buying one. Most people have ready access to some form of photocopying service, but shop around until you find a good one. Beware the high-street 'print shops'. They can be very expensive. The cheapest source is usually a small printer of the type one finds tucked away on trading estates.

Stationery and documents

Notepaper
The same people who say you will not be taken seriously by clients if you do not have an elaborate office, will also tell you that you must have high-quality, two-colour headed paper and printed envelopes. They are wrong. Simple, single-colour paper is all that is required. Clients will be impressed by what you have to say, not the paper you say it on. Many consultants simply create their letterheads using the software supplied with most PCs and print their letters directly onto plain paper. If you do have printed notepaper, make sure it is printed on the paper you use for the rest of your work so that things match up neatly.

Compliment slips
These are useful, but keep them simple and make sure they match letterheads and other stationery.

Cards
Cards can be very expensive, especially if they are complicated and in colour, so keep them simple. Again, check to see if your PC can produce acceptable cards using the precut blanks now readily available.

Invoices
When using a PC, there is little point in having specially printed invoices, especially if you have accounting software that generates a perfectly acceptable invoice when the relevant information is entered.

Reports, brochures etc.
On Friday we will look at the production of brochures and other public-relations (PR) material, but for printing these

and other key documents, two recommendations stand out from all others:

1 Keep all printed matter simple and businesslike.
2 Find a good printing company and use it for all your needs; including photocopying if it has the capacity and is readily accessible.

The business plan

There are some important financial plans that anyone setting up in business should prepare (these will be looked at on Thursday), but it is also vital to have a business plan that gives a clear picture of the consultancy's objectives and how these will be achieved.

This plan should set out:

• the services the consultancy intends to provide – these should be precisely identified and their relevance to client needs regularly reviewed

- the special benefits the consultancy can offer – by listing the particular strengths the consultancy possesses, especially those things in which it has an edge on its rivals, the marketing strategy will stay sharply focussed
- who the first clients will be – the consultancy does not exist until it has its first clients, and dealing with early clients will set important patterns for future strategy
- the way in which clients are to be serviced – this must be planned, and it should include:
    - *how* the service will be delivered (methods, style, reports, meetings etc.)
    - *what* will be delivered (the technical, practical and intellectual content)
- how new clients will be found – a basic marketing strategy is needed right from the start

Looking the part

There is probably more nonsense in the advice so freely given about what consultants should wear, and the sort of car they should drive, than on any other aspect of the profession.

Appearance
There is no standard way a consultant should dress, and the only rule worth remembering is to look right for the client.

- Do not arrive on a construction site dressed for a business meeting or turn up for a head office meeting dressed for a construction site.
- First impressions are important. If you are not sure of a potential client's dress habits, it is safer to dress 'up' rather than 'down' for the first meeting.

> The objective of appearance is really very simple:
> both you and the client should feel comfortable.

Car

Short of having a personal fleet of vehicles ranging from a
rusty old Land Rover to a gleaming new Rolls Royce, there
is no way you can meet everyone's expectation of what
constitutes the 'correct' sort of car for a consultant; so do
not try. All that is needed is a reliable vehicle that looks
well cared for. If there are clients out there who assess a
consultant's professional skill by the car he or she drives,
you would be well advised to avoid them.

What the client expects

The serious client will form an opinion about a consultant's
suitability for an assignment by deciding how well he or
she meets some (or all) of the following expectations:

- confidence
- authority
- a mature manner
- good listening skills
- a quick grasp of problems and ideas
- enthusiasm
- a helpful attitude

Note that these expectations are about *attitude* and
professionalism rather than appearance.

Paperwork

Becoming an independent consultant brings no relief from paperwork. Indeed, many of the tasks self-employed consultants have to do for themselves, which other people did for them when they were working in an organisation, involve paperwork.

Among the mass of letters, invoices, notes, bookkeeping entries and other more mundane paperwork, there are two writing jobs that rise in importance above all others:

1   *proposals* – the documents sent to clients in a bid to get work;
2   *reports* – the consultant's report is usually the final document the client receives; and often the only comprehensive and permanent record of what was achieved during the assignment.

Writing proposals
Most people, when writing the opening sections of a proposal, follow the well-established 'Rule of the Four Ps':

* **Position** – the current situation
* **Problem** – the issue that has to be tackled
* **Possibilities** – a summary of the various ways in which a solution might be found
* **Proposition** – the solution the consultant proposes

Applying this rule, and adding the other essential elements like cost, terms and conditions, timing etc., we get the following general structure for a proposal:

- an introduction which reviews the general situation, puts the subject of the proposal into perspective and demonstrates to potential clients the consultant's understanding of their organisation, its activities and its culture
- a clear statement of the consultant's perception of the problem, which also identifies the parameters within which a solution must be sought
- an evaluation of possible solutions, showing the positive and negative effects each solution would produce
- a detailed outline of the consultant's preferred solution (the proposal), with a carefully argued case for its adoption
- a section that sets out terms and conditions under which the consultant will undertake the assignment, the timing and length of the project and an indication of the cost

- a closing section with a summary of what has been proposed and the benefits it will provide for the client

Writing reports

At one time, almost every assignment was directed towards the submission of a report outlining the consultant's findings and recommendations. Today, very few assignments are so sharply focussed on recommendations and advice, but the report remains a key element in most assignments, and a consultant must be able to write reports that impress as well as inform and convince clients.

> A report is often the most tangible product of a consulting assignment, providing a record of results and recommendations that remains accessible long after the excitement and enthusiasm of the event is forgotten.

Reports are about answering questions

A prime function of most reports is to provide answers to questions. To produce a good report, the writer must know, or be able accurately to guess, the questions the reader will ask.

A good way to start preparing material for a report is to draw up a checklist of these questions. Of course, they will vary widely with each situation, but there are some broad, general questions that come up on almost every occasion. These include:

- What is the report supposed to achieve?
- What is it saying that is new?
- What (and who) will benefit from its recommendations?
- How does it affect me?

- Do we have the resources (people, equipment etc.)?
- How much will it cost?
- What are the consequences if we ignore the recommendations?

The effort and time spent completing this checklist, and devising answers to each question, will be rewarded both in the effectiveness of the finished report and in the ease with which it will be written.

Report structure

The secret of a good report is structure. Each consultant must develop a report structure that fits his or her personal style and meets the needs of the clients, but the general suggestions given below should provide a good starting point.

- *Introduction* – what the report is about
- *Objective* – what the assignment was intended to achieve, and the problems it addressed
- *Background* – any information that puts the assignment into context (why it was requested, by whom etc.)
- *The findings* – details of the information and opinions gathered during the assignment
- *Views* – the consultant's opinion of what the findings imply, and the conclusions he or she has drawn from them
- *Recommendations* – the consultant's recommendations for action

The quality of the writing
The writing, layout and presentation of a consulting
assignment report is important, and especially so with
those clients who feel (quite wrongly in most cases) that the
report is what they paid all that money for.

A report that is well written and easy to read is also a
powerful promotion document. Reports find their way to
senior managers in parent and associated organisations.
When read by such people, who will have had no direct
involvement in the work it records, a report is the only
measure they have of the consultant's skill and knowledge.
As these are likely to be the people who will decide if you
are to be asked to undertake further assignments, it is
worth the effort of polishing up the wording and layout for
this reason alone.

Drafting and revision

There is little genius but a lot of hard work needed to produce a well-written report. If your personal writing skills are not as good as you would like them to be, seek help, but few people fail to write good reports because they lack basic writing skills. The usual reason for writing badly is lack of effort. The worst reports are those the writer thinks are finished at the first draft. Nobody is that good. Most of us need to go through several revisions before a report is presentable.

> If you can produce a good report in less than two redrafts you are far too bright to be in this business.

Summary

Today we have looked at the material requirements of a consultancy, the business plan, image requirements, and the paperwork involved.

Getting started

Today we are looking at a number of legal and business management issues. These include:

- What kind of business (company, partnership etc.)?
- Naming the consultancy
- Insurance
- Employing others
- Contracts and agreements
- Terms and conditions

What kind of business?

Becoming a consultant involves setting up a business, and an early problem for every new consultant is to decide what kind of business to establish. Essentially there are only three possibilities: to become a sole trader, a partnership or a limited company.

Sole trader

Becoming a sole trader is the simplest way for a self-employed person to establish a business. Setting up a sole-trader business, or to use its up-market title, a sole proprietorship, involves no complicated legal processes, and there are no fees or charges. All that is needed to establish such a business is to tell your local tax inspector and DSS office that you intend to become self-employed. These offices will ask you to complete a few simple forms and then organise your tax assessment and DSS payments.

Partnership

Obviously, a partnership will only be an option if you intend to involve other people in the business. Partners are generally of two types:

1 *full partners*, who share the profits (and losses) and take part in the management and operations of the business;
2 *sleeping partners*, who have a financial interest in the business but take no part in its management.

A partnership is a more complicated form of business than a sole proprietorship and the various roles and responsibilities of the people involved need to be clearly identified. A legal document known as a *Partnership Agreement* is required to establish these relationships and allocate responsibility among the partners. This document should be prepared by a solicitor.

Limited company

This is the most complicated of the three types of business a consultant might decide to establish, and it has as its main benefit the concept of *limited liability*. A limited company must be registered at Companies House, and it has to appoint directors, prepare memoranda and articles of association, file accounts annually, have a registered office with the name displayed on the outside and satisfy many other requirements.

Being a limited company offers few benefits to an independent consultant working alone, but once a consultancy begins to grow and employ staff, the situation is quite different. Forming a company is then strongly advised for the important protection it offers should there be a dramatic change in the company's affairs. It also makes it easier for a consultancy to raise capital, establish relations with other companies and increase client confidence.

Which to choose?
Unless there are clear technical or legal reasons for doing otherwise, anyone starting out as an independent consultant is usually advised to settle for the simplest form of business and become a sole trader.

Naming the consultancy

Choosing the right name for a consultancy is not an easy task. And once a consultancy is named and clients get used to it, changing the name can be a damaging exercise. To get it right first time, it may be worth considering the following points and suggestions:

- Keep the name simple, preferably no more than three words.
- Take care with service or product names. These can be restrictive and may make it difficult for the consultancy to move into new fields ('Farndale Quality Management Consultants' may have marketing problems when trying to offer employment law advice).

- Avoid regional names as these may make it difficult for a consultant to work outside the named region ('East Sussex Management' may have problems selling its services outside of south-east England).
- Do not get too carried away with grand-sounding names ('Knightsbridge Global Management' will frighten off more potential clients than it will attract).

The majority of consultants use their own name in their consultancy's title. If a consultant intends staying in the same area of activity, a word describing this activity can be used to complement the consultant's name, e.g. 'Frank Lunn Marketing', 'Jane Milburn Recruiting'. A consultant wishing to range widely, or avoid being pinned down to a specialism, can simply add the word 'associates', e.g. 'Jean Anderson Associates'. This does not carry any commitment to have associates, but it makes it easy to bring in others to help when needed and it places no restriction on the fields in which the consultancy might operate. It also sounds businesslike and professional.

If using the proprietor's name is not acceptable for any reason, then a service-related name may be considered, e.g. 'Production Management Solutions', 'Effective Employee Communications'. The problem here is that the limited number of words to choose from increases the risk of selecting a name already being used by another consultant. With no national register of consultancy names, the problem of duplication, and the confusion it can cause, is hard to avoid.

A more common solution is to use some neutral words, like the name of a house or an animal, e.g. 'Park Lodge Consultants', 'Mallard Associates'.

Logos

It is best to avoid logos until you are well established and have a clear idea of the image you wish to project. The simplest and most common logo is one formed from the initial letters of the consultancy's name. For instance, the logo of 'John Frankland Associates' would be 'JFA'.

Bold or stylised initials followed by a qualifying description can look rather smart:

JFA
Management Development Consultants

Insurance

Insurance for a sole trader is fairly straightforward. For advice on insuring equipment and personal things like life insurance, permanent health insurance (this pays some income if you are too ill to work), medical insurance etc., seek the help of a reputable insurance broker. Your bank manager or accountant will be able to recommend someone.

If working from home, check with your house insurers and mortgage lenders to make certain they are happy with the arrangement. Check also with your car insurers to ensure that you are fully covered when using your car for business purposes.

Insurance for partnerships and limited companies is more complicated, and the advice of a lawyer, accountant or specialist broker will be needed.

Professional indemnity insurance

Perhaps the most important consideration for a consultant is professional indemnity insurance. This covers the consultant against claims from a client for damage caused by negligence, bad advice or misconduct. Indemnity insurance can be expensive, so before approaching a broker have a word with any professional body of which you are a member. Many professional bodies have schemes offering indemnity insurance to members at discount rates.

Employing others

Support staff

When first setting up in business, few consultants will be employing staff. Those who do require full-time or part-time assistance are recommended to seek the advice of a solicitor, accountant or one of the many agencies providing practical help to new businesses. Employing staff is a complex business, and we cannot hope to cover all the details in this general introduction to running a consultancy.

When a consultancy begins to get busy, and help is needed, the consultant should first make sure that employing someone *is* the best and most cost-effective solution. In their formative years, most consultants make maximum use of specialist firms and agencies to help with clerical work, mail shots, telephone answering etc. Employing staff should only be considered when it becomes the cheapest option and there are clear indications that the additional workload is going to be permanent.

Associates
Long before they need the support of permanent office staff, most consultants encounter situations where they require additional consulting help. This may be because a job is so large it needs more than one person to carry out the work, or more commonly, because some aspect of the project requires specialist knowledge and skills that the consultant does not possess. Bringing in another consultant to help in this way is not employing someone; all that is happening is that part of the work is being shared with another person or firm.

Contracts and agreements

When dealing with small consultants, most clients do not require lengthy, formal contracts and prefer simple written agreements that follow a more or less standard format. When the terms are agreed, the consultant provides two signed copies of the agreement, both of which the client signs, returning one copy to the consultant.

Whilst simple in form, such an exchange of letters constitutes a legal contract, and any breach or failure to comply by either party could end in a court action.

Types of contract
Most contracts fall into three categories:

1 *fixed-price contracts* – to carry out a specific assignment for an agreed overall price;
2 *variable-price contracts* – to charge an agreed rate (usually a daily rate) for work completed;
3 *retainer contracts* – to work a specific number of days (or provide a particular service) each month, year or some other specified period, for an agreed fee paid at regular intervals.

What to include in the contract
The contract or agreement should reflect the consultant's terms and conditions of working (see the next section below on terms and conditions) and cover the following key points:

• The objective of the assignment and the specific tasks to be carried out will be stated.
• Variable-price contracts must have an estimate of the time the assignment will take and an agreed minimum and maximum price based on the daily rate.
• Fixed-price contracts usually include an estimate of the number of days the assignment will take and show how the price relates to this estimate.
• Retainer contracts normally specify the number of days to be worked each month, the number of months for which the contract will run and the agreed monthly fee.

- All contracts will normally include a starting date and a
  completion date. Make sure these dates are realistic
  and achievable by *both you and the client* before signing.
  When a project is going to be lengthy, complex or likely
  to be affected by things beyond your control, insist on a
  completion date that is conditional.
- Specify the expenses that will be added to the total cost
  and any agreed rates for things like car mileage,
  accommodation, materials, equipment hire etc.

Terms and conditions

It is essential that a consultancy prepare a detailed
statement of the terms and conditions under which it is
prepared to do business. Relevant parts of this statement
will be routinely included in contracts and proposals and
may form part of the promotional material sent to
prospective clients.

Each consultant is going to add points relating to his or her specialism and personal requirements, but the following example of a simple set of terms and conditions may help as a basic outline.

Terms and Conditions of Working

1 Fees

Fees for assignments will be agreed before any work begins and charged in one of two ways:

1.1 Daily rate – a fee per consultant/day to be agreed in advance and maintained throughout the period of the assignment. Either a fixed number of days will be agreed for the assignment or, where the nature of the assignment makes it impossible to estimate accurately the time required, a minimum and maximum length will be agreed. Should the consultant take longer than the agreed maximum number of days to complete the assignment, the extra time will *not* be charged to the client.

The consultant retains the right to negotiate a new rate for any subsequent assignments.

1.2 Fixed price – as an alternative to charging on a daily basis the client may prefer to agree with the consultant a fixed price for completing an assignment. Once agreed, this contract price will be binding on the consultant so long as the client does not alter the terms and requirements.

NB: all such contracts and agreements will be in writing.

---

2 Material

Equipment, and any written material needed, will be provided by the Consultant. The cost of providing this material, and of preparing reports and presentation documents, will be covered by the assignment fee unless otherwise agreed.

3 Invoices

Unless alternative arrangements are agreed, invoices will be submitted at the end of each calendar month for the work completed by that date. Payment will be due within 14 days of the invoice date.

4 Variations

If, after the details of an assignment have been agreed with the Consultant, the Client decides to vary these in any way, the Consultant reserves the right to renegotiate the fee for the assignment and the time needed to complete it.

5 Travelling expenses

The consultant's travel will be by first-class rail, business-class air or car as seems appropriate. Car mileage will be charged at the current AA mileage rates.

6 Accommodation

Where overnight accommodation and meals are necessary, these may be provided by the Client at a standard which is appropriate. When the Consultant makes the accommodation arrangements, these will be charged to the Client at cost.

Training work
Consultants who provide training services may find the
following example helpful. It replaces the first five
paragraphs in the above example with training-related
terms and conditions.

Terms and Conditions of Working (Training)

1   Cancellation
Cancellation of a course cannot be accepted after a
date 30 days prior to the agreed commencement
date. If a course is cancelled during this period, the
fee will be payable in full. If cancellation is received in
writing more than 30 days before the commencement
date, then a cancellation charge will be made
according to the following scale:

Number of days notice:	Cancellation charge:
30–60 days	50% of total fee
60–90 days	20% of total fee

To these cancellation charges will be added any
material and labour costs incurred up to the date of
cancellation.

2   Equipment
All notes, case studies, videos and other course
material will be provided by the Consultancy. The cost
of this material will be covered by the course fee
unless otherwise stated. Where overhead projectors,
screens, video equipment etc. are not available at the
venue, these can be supplied or hired by the
Consultancy and charged to the Client at cost.

---

3   Invoices

Invoices will be submitted immediately on completion of each course, with payment due within 14 days of the last day of the training.

4   Deferrals

If a Client wishes to defer a course to a date which is more than six months after the original agreed date, or on an indefinite basis, this will be regarded as a cancellation, and the provisions in Clause 1 will apply.

If a Client would like to defer a course to a date which is less than six months from the agreed date, then the Client will be liable immediately for 50% of the agreed fee, with the remaining 50% payable on completion at the new date.

5   Variations

If, after a programme has been agreed with the Consultancy, the Client decides to vary this in any way, the Consultancy reserves the right to make a charge for any additional costs involved.

Summary

Today we have looked at different types of business, choosing a name, insurance, employing others, contracts and agreements, and terms and conditions.

Money

Today we are looking at the financial side of running a consultancy. The issues covered include:

- budgeting
- bookkeeping
- choosing and using an accountant
- tax
- VAT
- fees
- expenses
- invoicing
- late payment
- bad debts

Budgeting

Many people find that the most frightening part of setting up in business for oneself is the disappearance of the regular monthly pay cheque. Even if a consultant is able to start working with a client on the first day in business, it could still be two or even three months before the first money comes in. To cope with the time lag between work and payment, and the unavoidable irregularity of consulting income, the newly established consultant should do two things:

1   make sure there is an adequate sum of money available to cover business expenses and living costs for the period between start-up and the first cheque arriving;
2   devise a budgeting system that will ensure cash is always available for essential outgoings and living costs despite the income fluctuations that are an inherent feature of consulting work.

The required budgeting system need not be complex or involve more than making a careful estimate of the money needed to pay the regular business and living expenses and setting this aside for the next two months as a rolling budget that cannot be 'raided' for any purpose whatsoever.

Bookkeeping

What accounts will you need?
The nature of consulting work means that the bookkeeping involved is much simpler than it is for say a retailer of equivalent size. Instead of hundreds of transactions a day, the consultant may only have half-a-dozen per month.

Overhead costs involve only a few regular bills and there is no significant purchasing of raw materials or outside services.

To keep track of the business and compile the information needed for tax returns, only two essential records are required during the early stages of building up a consultancy:

1 a monthly account showing income and expenditure;
2 an annual account which brings together the monthly accounts and adds any annual items to provide a complete picture of the business turnover, expenses and profit.

Monthly account
The monthly account is best done as a simple spreadsheet in which each column carries information relating to an item of income or expenditure. The layout of a typical monthly account is shown below:

Columns 1 to 6 (Information and charges)					
1	2	3	4	5	6
Date	Client	Invoice no	Sale (+VAT)	Sale (less VAT)	Fee

Notes

Invoice number – a unique reference number for every invoice (see the later section on invoicing)

Sale – the total amount charged to the client, plus VAT if the consultancy is registered (see the later section on VAT)

Sale (less VAT) – if relevant

Fee – the fee element of the invoice

Columns 7 to 10 (Assignment expenses)

7	8	9	10
Train	Mileage	Car expenses	Accommodation/meals

Notes

Mileage – the number of miles travelled and charged to the client

Car expenses – miles travelled multiplied by the rate charged per mile (this rate per mile is that agreed with the Inland Revenue and may be different from the amount paid by the client)

Columns 11 to 13 (General expenses)

11	12	13
Office expenses	Post	Miscellaneous

Notes

Office expenses – stationery, printing, reference books, computer material etc.

Miscellaneous – any items such as equipment, office furniture etc. that do not fit into any of the other categories

Monthly expenses

Each month there will be expenses for items in columns 11 to 13 that do not relate directly to a specific assignment. There will also be travel and car expenses (do not forget car parking) and occasionally meals and accommodation. These expenses are best set out on a separate sheet for each month, all receipts being carefully checked and stapled to the sheet before the relevant totals are transferred as an additional horizontal line in the monthly account.

Annual accounts
These accounts are similar in layout to the monthly accounts. They use the same column headings into which the totals for each month are entered plus any other quarterly or annual amounts that fall due. This account 'rolls' forward giving a detailed picture of the current state and progress of the business. At the end of 12 months, it provides all the basic business information needed for tax and other purposes.

Choosing and using an accountant

Why use an accountant?
Anyone planning to set up a serious consulting business is advised to seek the services of a qualified accountant. As well as providing valuable advice on all aspects of financial management, an accountant can frequently help a consultancy organise its affairs in ways that will save significant amounts of money.

Finding a good accountant
When looking for a suitable accountant, seek the advice of your bank manager, any small business agency that is helping you and anyone who is already running a similar business locally and whose opinion you can trust.

The most important thing to remember when choosing an accountant is:

> Never go for someone who has not been personally recommended and who is not professionally qualified.

Using your accountant
Accountants are not just there to fill in your tax returns and sort out errors in your bookkeeping. They are professional business advisors who can be especially valuable during the early years of a consultancy's existence. Seek their advice, listen to their counsel, but remember always that it is *your* business and that *you* are finally responsible for every decision that is made.

Tax

Sole traders
Self-employed consultants operating as sole traders
normally pay tax in two instalments: the first in January and
the second in July. This comes as a sharp contrast to the
experience of previously employed people whose tax was
deducted monthly by their employer under a PAYE system.

The way the Inland Revenue calculates a sole trader's tax is
not significantly different from the income-tax system an
employed person is familiar with: the same escalating rates
apply according to the amount earned, and the usual
family and other allowances are permitted. The key
difference is in establishing the amount earned – that is to
say, the money that is left when all the permitted expenses
and allowances have been deducted.

> Knowing what expenses are allowed, and calculating
> the exact amount on which tax must be paid, can be a
> problem; the skilled advice of an accountant or tax
> advisor can make the task a lot easier.

Allowable expenses
The following checklist includes most of the expenses
normally regarded as allowable:

- office expenses – telephone, postage, printing,
  stationery etc.
- rent and rates – if you work from home, a contribution
  to home expenses will be allowed.
- professional expenses – relevant books, journals,
  training courses, subscriptions to professional bodies etc.

- travel and subsistence – when wholly work-related.
- car – a car can be bought as part of the business, or a family car can be used from time to time for business needs. The arrangement chosen will depend mainly on the amount of car travel involved. When a car is part of the business and also used for private motoring, the tax arrangements must be negotiated with your tax inspector. If a private car is used for business travel, the Inland Revenue allows a generous rate of tax relief for the first 4,000 miles travelled in the tax year and rather less for travel in excess of 4,000 miles.
- support – the cost of employing one's spouse or partner to help in the business is allowable providing he or she is genuinely employed and paid at the market rate.
- bank charges – on business accounts only.
- accounting and audit fees.
- interest – the interest on loans and overdrafts for the business (and the cost of arranging them).
- business insurance.

Partnership
The tax calculations in partnerships can be highly complex as they depend on how the profit is divided between partners and the total taxable income of each partner. Anyone contemplating a partnership arrangement is advised to take professional advice.

Limited company
The tax arrangements for a company are very different from those for sole traders and partnerships. Corporate tax replaces income and capital gains tax, and the directors and any additional staff are paid a salary by the company and this is taxed in the normal way for an employed person.

Again, professional advice is needed to navigate a way through the many complexities of corporate taxation.

VAT

The details of this complex tax are beyond the scope of this book, but there are some excellent guides available both from Customs and Excise, who administer VAT (value added tax), and from other agencies.

The main problem for a consultant starting out is the decision to register for VAT. Any business can register for VAT, but it is not required to do so if its turnover is less than an annually agreed figure – currently (1998/99) £50,000. For businesses using large amounts of raw materials and bought-in services, this figure is quickly reached, but in a one-person consultancy, where materials and overheads are only a small part of the overall turnover, a respectable living can be made before this limit is reached. There is an added advantage of not being registered if the consultancy is likely to service clients who would not be able to recover the VAT added to their bills.

An important benefit from being VAT-registered is the recovery of the VAT on equipment and services purchased for the business. If significant amounts of material and equipment have to be bought, registration would have obvious benefits, and 'voluntary' registration may be the right option, even if turnover is well below the point at which it becomes mandatory.

Fees

Until a consultant is well established and has developed a good 'feel' for the market, deciding what fee to ask of a potential client is not easy. In some specialist areas, there may be a recognised 'going rate', but in general there are large variations in the fees consultants charge.

Clients will take into account the lower overheads and costs of a small consultancy and expect your fees to be lower than those of a larger firm, but do not be tempted to charge fees that are too low. Cut-price rates will not necessarily bring in business; indeed, many clients equate low charges with poor quality. Also, remember that you are in business to make a living, and low prices produce low income.

Expenses

Many consultants do themselves harm by keeping their fee
low and loading the expenses. Clients do not like open-
ended arrangements, and most will insist on knowing
exactly what they will have to pay in total and how that
sum is to be made up.

Unless expensive materials are needed, or manuals are to
be written and printed, there is a good case for including
everything in the price apart from obvious variable
expenses like travel and accommodation. This
straightforward approach is a good selling point, and the
client might settle for a slightly higher price if they know
that it is the maximum they will have to pay and there will
be no nasty surprises.

Invoicing

A well-designed invoice should provide:

* *the client* with a brief but clear description of the work
  carried out during the period in question, the charge for
  each element (daily fee or agreed price) and the
  expenses incurred (with receipts or some other proof
  of payment)
* *the consultant* with the information needed to complete
  accounts easily (the date, client, sale, fee element,
  invoice number etc.)

Invoice number
There is value in having a code numbering system for
invoices. This makes for easy reference on the part of both
consultant and client. Most consultancies develop a system

that reflects their special needs but a good place to start is with a simple three-part reference. The three parts of the reference are:

1 *the client reference* – usually a two-letter abbreviation of the client organisation's name;
2 *the invoice number* – each invoice being numbered in order of issue, starting at the beginning of each 12 month accounting period or calendar year;
3 *the year* – again, the choice can be either the financial year or the calendar year.

Using this method, the third in a series of invoices sent to one Fred Arkroyd Mills in 1999 would be coded:

FA/3/99

Invoice layout
The example below shows an invoice layout that meets all the points we have just discussed and provides a clear and presentable document that a client will find easy to process.

Jean Anderson Associates   Willowbrook
Management Development Consultants   Midge Lane
                                                         Peghampton
                                                         ZZ19 9NW
                                                         Tel: 0123 456

INVOICE FA/3/99   3 June 1999
Fred Arkroyd Mills
1 Canal Row
Smeltville

Re: <u>Staff Appraisal Programme</u> – 1. Head Office presentation
                                                        26 May
                                              2. Factory Course 28 May

    <u>Fee</u>:
    Two days @ £500 per Day   £1,000.00

    <u>Expenses</u>
    Meeting in London 26 May 1999
       Train: (Peghampton to Waterloo)   £21.99
       Car Park: £2.50
       Car: 10 mls @ 34p per mile   £3.40

    Course at Smeltville 28 May 1999
       Car: 288 mls @ 34p per mile   £97.92

    TOTAL   £1,125.81

Payment due within 15 days of the date of this invoice

When to invoice

For most routine assignments, the common practice is to invoice at the end of each month for the work carried out during that month.

For major assignments, especially if they involve a lot of research and preparation, there is a good argument for requesting some part-payment of both fees and expenses in advance. Naturally this must be negotiated as part of the overall contract, but most clients will regard such a request as reasonable.

Late payment

It is a sad fact that many organisations are slow to pay their debts to small businesses.

There are two strategies that will help reduce the problem of late payment:

1 Decide what payment arrangements you feel are reasonable (e.g. payment within 28 days) and make this clear a) in your proposal, b) in the agreement you sign and c) at the bottom of each invoice (see the invoice example above)
2 Be firm and act quickly with anyone who runs over the agreed time limit; if payment is not received by an agreed date a reminder or statement should be sent *immediately*. Statements that arrive two weeks after a payment is due suggest that you are not too worried about the money. Statements that arrive hours after payment is due show that you mean business.

Pressing for payment
There are people who will say that you should not press for payment as this will upset the client and you could lose future business. This has to be another myth. Accounts departments decide when invoices are paid; the person with whom you are dealing is much more likely to be embarrassed to hear that you have been inconvenienced than affronted by a request for something that was promised.

Bad debts

Most consultants report few bad debts, but from time to time organisations will refuse to pay for some reason, or else disappear without paying, and the consultant has a problem. If the amount of money is substantial, then seek legal advice, but if it is not too great then take a philosophical view. By all means try hard to get what is due to you, but take care that the cost of recovery does not become greater than the sum you are trying to recover. If the cost of recovering a debt, including the indirect cost of lost time and energy, does become too much, it may be best to walk away from it. There is one small consolation: bad debts are tax-deductible.

Summary

Today we have looked at all the financial aspects: budgeting, bookkeeping, using an accountant, tax, VAT, fees, expenses, invoices, late payments and bad debts.

Promoting and marketing

Today we are looking at how best to promote and present a consultancy to potential clients. Issues examined include:

- marketing and selling consulting services
- the brochure and other promotional literature
- presentations to potential clients
- advertising and PR

Marketing and selling consulting services

The line marking the difference between marketing and selling, so clear in the manufacturing and retail industries, becomes fuzzy as it enters the service sector, and all but disappears when it gets to consulting.

Consulting services have to be sold, but the 'sell' is a fairly obvious operation at the end of a subtle marketing exercise.

From time to time, organisations hit problems and go in search of a suitable consultant, but most prefer to be aware of what a range of consultants has to offer so they can produce a shortlist of potential providers whenever some need arises. To have a chance of being on these shortlists, a consultancy must be known to as many organisations as possible.

Getting its services known to would-be clients is a consultancy's main marketing task.

Why this consultancy?

Being known to potential clients is vital, but the next most important thing is to be selected from among all the other 'known' consultants. As we learned on Sunday, there are a small number of key factors that influence organisations when they are making their final selection.

The top three of these factors are the consultant's:

1 understanding of the client's needs
2 personal qualities
3 specialist knowledge.

Whilst a consultant's competence in these three areas is more easily demonstrated in a face-to-face encounter with a potential client, every effort should be made to show an understanding of them in correspondence and promotion literature. It is hard to put over in writing subjective things like a concern for client needs or someone's personal qualities, but the skill must be mastered if a consultancy is to prosper.

Simply telling a potential client that a particular service is part of your consultancy's repertoire is not enough. Organisations need to be convinced that when handling the assignment you will:

- show an understanding of their needs and not simply sell them a ready-made solution
- be both willing and able to adapt your methods and strategy to fit into each client's corporate culture and way of doing things
- bring to the assignment a significant degree of specialist knowledge and skill

How much time and effort is required?

The books and articles offering advice to would-be consultants are littered with widely differing instructions on how they should divide their time between servicing existing clients and finding new ones. This confusion is easily explained: only *you* can judge what is best for your own business. If clients are knocking at the door pleading for help, the need for marketing is going to feel less urgent than when the order book is nearly empty. The problem is not one of finding a neat formula to calculate time allocation; it is a matter of striking the right balance between making a good job of the tasks in hand and putting enough time and effort into making sure there are new jobs in the pipeline.

The most common problem is not spending enough time seeking new business. All too many fledgling consultants throw themselves energetically into their first assignment and give no thought to where the next job will come from.

Finding new assignments can take months, and it has to be a process that goes on in parallel with even the most demanding assignments.

If you do not start looking for new clients until your current assignments are complete, you could spend long periods without work.

Marketing is a constant task

Marketing and promoting your consultancy are tasks that you neglect at your peril. One very successful consultant, when asked for a useful marketing tip, said that he had a personal rule that he must do some marketing task every day, irrespective of how busy he was. This could be something as simple as a single phone call during a brief interlude in a hectic 15-hour day or the revision of a major promotion document whilst on a long train journey. 'The secret', he said, 'is to do *something* every day and never be deflected.'

Marketing and promotion policy

When deciding what your marketing and promotion policy will be, it may be helpful to keep the following points in mind:

- Never lose sight of the need to market and promote your services, no matter how busy you might be
- Make sure that your enthusiasm to satisfy current clients does not take attention away from the need constantly to seek new ones
- Exploit every opportunity to gain the interest of those who are potential clients
- Continually update and improve your promotional material by incorporating the experience gained from working with clients

- During the early years, when your consultancy is finding its feet, be prepared to spend more time on promoting your services than on delivering them

Get the balance right
As your consultancy becomes more established, take care to monitor the balance between servicing clients and marketing. Disaster awaits those who:

- *because they neglect their marketing*, have excellent services but no clients, or
- *because they neglect the quality of their services*, have plenty of clients but are unable to service them well.

The brochure and other promotional literature

Every consultancy needs some kind of general brochure to use for large-scale distribution and in response to casual enquiries. Producing such a brochure is another of those exercises where it is all too easy to spend a lot of money for little or no gain. There are those who say a new consultancy cannot get off the ground without first amazing the market with a glossy brochure filled with colour photographs of earnest-looking men and women in designer clothes passing on their wisdom to clients who appear entranced by what they are hearing. This has to be wrong. Few organisations are taken in by colourful literature, especially when seeking professional advice on important issues.

Yes, the big consulting firms do have rather grand brochures, but this has more to do with keeping in step with their rivals than with real marketing. The small consultancy, targeting a narrow, specialist field, would raise more suspicion than interest if it started sending out expensively produced material. What seems appropriate for the small consultancy are simple, attractive, well-written documents that contain precisely the information a prospective client would like to know.

Small can be beautiful
The one-person consultancy has a distinct advantage over larger firms by having just one individual to market. The one-person consultancy brochure can be very directly written to reflect what that person has to offer and the experience on which his or her skill and knowledge is based.

A one-person consultancy brochure
The contents of such a brochure should put over the following four key pieces of information:

1 a general statement identifying the subjects in which the consultant specialises and the background from which he or she has gained the necessary experience;

2   a list (not too long) of the services the consultancy can
    provide;
3   an honest account, without being too bashful or too
    boastful, of the consultant's relevant experience,
    qualifications and achievements;
4   a list of the sectors in which the consultant feels
    equipped to operate and the level of personnel that he or
    she can help.

For consultants who are just starting out, the content of the
first and third sections will be based largely on
employment experience. After carrying out a few
assignments, these sections can be rewritten to reflect their
consulting experience. Similarly, the fourth section will
shift in time from a list of areas in which they would like to
work, to a list of those in which they have worked.

> This simple format can produce a convincing
> document that provides all the information needed to
> attract the attention of potential clients.

The brochure layout
The above four-part format lends itself to two useful layouts:

• Layout 1: with careful editing, it can form a single-page
             A4 document which is easily and cheaply
             produced on a PC. This version is handy for
             the casual inquirer and for inclusion in papers
             handed out at meetings or seminars.

- Layout 2: the full version should fit neatly into a three-fold in which the key information occupies the inner three pages, with the outside carrying a front cover and a rear page listing the areas in which the consultancy operates and details like the address, telephone and fax numbers.

Support documents

Once the brochure is prepared, it becomes a simple matter to supplement it with a range of items that describe specific services in greater detail or specially written notes for use when approaching organisations whose needs are known. Add to these reprints of any publicity the consultancy has received plus articles written by or about the consultancy and there is enough material to make up some impressive packs to use in response to enquiries or to send to organisations identified as likely clients.

Presentation

Clients who hire consultants without first meeting them are both rare and very foolish. This means that once a client is interested in what you have to offer, they will want to see you. Normally, this means a meeting with one or two people, but increasingly clients are asking for formal presentations.

If a formal presentation is requested, all the things we looked at on Monday will apply, but even if the request is for a simple meeting, many of the presentation skills will still be relevant. After all, you are being asked to present your ideas, and whilst this may not involve making a speech, you would be well advised to follow the checklist on page 29 when arranging your material and preparing for the meeting.

When asked to make a formal presentation, make every effort to find out how much time you have, what sort of room you will be in, what equipment will be available and how many people will be attending. Turning up with a 30-minute presentation designed for a large audience and using a slide or overhead projector is going to give you problems when the client first says that you only have 10 minutes and then shows you into a small room in which there are three people and no facilities for visual aids.

Advertising and PR

Another temptation when starting out as a consultant is to advertise one's services in some appropriate magazine or journal. This is rarely a good idea. Advertising is expensive, and there are few indications that organisations seeking consulting services take much notice of advertisements. There are exceptions for consultants operating in highly specialised fields and those with new and innovative ideas, but for most consultants the response to an advertisement is unlikely to justify the cost. What it will produce is a sharp increase in your junk mail and a plague of calls from salespersons.

If advertising is going to stretch the budget, the very thought of using a public-relations (PR) agency would bring immediate financial ruin. Of course, no one is going to suggest that a small consultancy should make use of a PR specialist; but there are several PR skills, like copywriting, presentation and media relations, about which a good consultant should be aware. It makes sense, therefore, to glean what one can from people in the PR business and take every opportunity, through reading and training, to develop the relevant PR skills.

Summary

Tomorrow we will look at some direct ways of approaching potential clients, but this general look at promoting and marketing can best be summed up by saying that every new consultancy must:

- take seriously the need to promote and market its services; making sure that enough time and energy are available for the task, no matter how busy the consultancy might be on current projects
- establish a marketing and promotional policy and follow it unerringly
- put care and effort into preparing and continuously revising promotional material
- ensure that all marketing and promotional material is simple in its presentation, flawless in its wording, accurate in its descriptions and sharply focussed on client needs
- take every opportunity to improve the quality of its promotional activity by improving existing marketing and PR skills and learning new ones

Winning new business

Today we are looking at how a consultancy might go about finding the steady supply of clients it needs to survive and the actions it should take to ensure continuing success and future growth.

These include:

- sources of new business
- networking
- cold-calling
- meeting potential clients
- newsletters
- growing the business
- finding the right niche
- providing a quality service

Sources of new business

First clients
For a high proportion of new consultants, the first client is their former employer. Other common sources are:

• contacts made whilst in employment
• introductions by friends and ex-colleagues
• people the consultant has met at professional or trade-association meetings

These early sources are very important in getting the consultancy off the ground, but most are 'one-off' opportunities and cannot be relied on to provide long-term business. To ensure a constant supply of clients, a consultancy must devise a systematic strategy for finding them.

New clients
To be sure of success, a consultancy must exploit every means of finding new business, but the experience of most small consulting firms would suggest that new clients come mainly from two sources:

1 personal recommendations by existing clients
2 networking.

Personal recommendations
This has to be the most satisfactory way of getting new clients, and we must never forget that a small job done well can lead to a recommendation for a much bigger job with another client.

Networking

This word has been much overused in recent years, and its meaning is now a little blurred for some people. Its use in the context of finding new business can best be defined as making the maximum use of existing contacts and actively generating new ones.

Perhaps we should say maximum effective use of contacts. Pestering people for work is not what we are talking about.

> Good networking is about keeping in touch with everyone you know who could help you find work and making sure they are well informed about what you can do and what you are doing.

Expanding your network
Extending a network of contacts is a demanding task, but one that is well worth the effort. New 'members' for your network will come from a variety of formal and informal sources.

Formal sources include:

- *professional bodies* – make the effort to attend branch meetings, AGMs and other events where likely users of your services will be present.
- *trade associations* – attend conferences and exhibitions and meet as many people as possible.
- *chambers of commerce, business clubs and other local business groups* – the value of local agencies will depend on the nature of your services. If what you have to offer is of interest to small businesses, they can provide valuable introductions.

Informal sources include:

- *friends, neighbours and family*
- *Sports and social gatherings*
- *anywhere where you might run into the right people* – many consultants claim to have won major contracts as the result of the most casual encounters in airport lounges and train dining cars.

Make networking productive

- Always carry business cards and basic promotional literature whenever there is the slightest chance of a useful encounter.
- Get people to talk about themselves and what they need rather than immediately telling them what you have to offer.
- Make notes on *every* encounter, however unpromising it might seem at the time. When someone gets in touch three months after you met them to say they would like to follow up an idea you raised, it can be rather embarrassing if you have no recollection of the meeting or what you talked about.

Recording network encounters
How you record the information gained from fleeting
encounters is immaterial; *what matters is that you record it.*
In particular, you must note down individuals' names,
addresses, telephone numbers, organisation details and
what you talked about.

Some people use printed forms to record details of the
people they meet. These can be easily filled in and
subsequently filed and cross-referenced. Others use the
ubiquitous 'Filofax' with its prepared stationery. One
highly successful head of a professional organisation used a
much less formal system. At the beginning of each day, he
filled the right-hand pocket of his jacket with small scraps
of paper on which he wrote the details of anything that
took his interest during the day, transferring each
completed note to his left-hand jacket pocket. At the end of
the day, the contents of the left-hand jacket pocket were
turned out and carefully read. Many of these notes went
straight into the waste bin, but the useful ones were then
transferred to a well-designed system of files and card
indexes.

Cold-calling

No one would contemplate trying to sell consulting services
by going around knocking on doors, so the only form of
cold-calling a consultant is likely to use is the mail shot.

Mail shots
The first thing one must accept about mail shots is their
poor response rate. This can be improved by:

- targeting the right organisations
- getting to the right people in the organisation
- personalising the letters
- making sure the contents of the letter relate to the recipient's likely needs
- keeping the wording of each letter short, to the point and positive in tone

Do not try to do too much in a letter. The objective is *not* to sell your services; no organisation is going to buy anything on the basis of a single unsolicited letter. A mail shot is intended simply to raise sufficient interest for the recipient to want to see you and talk. The selling cannot begin until you have met people from the organisation, talked to them, identified their problems and worked out some solutions.

Many people follow up each unanswered letter with a telephone call. Whilst some claim that such calls have resulted in meetings that would not otherwise have taken place, the incidence of this is rare and one needs to be sure the time and cost involved in making a large number of calls can be justified. Follow-up telephone calls can also be counter-productive. If an organisation is interested in what you have to offer, they will get in touch, but not necessarily immediately they receive your letter, and a follow-up telephone call may be regarded as a hard sell that actually puts them off.

> There are divided views about the value of follow-up telephone calls and much will depend on the culture into which a consultant is marketing.

Mailing lists

Most consultants start out with a well-prepared list of likely clients whom they know about from personal contact. Such lists are very important, and often provide early and valuable clients, but they must be extended to include as many potential client organisations as possible. This task is not as onerous as it may sound, thanks to the many excellent directories now available that list organisations according to the nature of their business and the sectors in which they operate. These directories are rather expensive, and quickly get out of date, but as they are widely available in public libraries, trade and professional-body libraries and places like business link, business clubs and chambers of commerce, few consultants feel the need to purchase them.

As well as names and addresses, these directories provide valuable information about an organisation's size, range of activities and who owns it.

Meeting potential clients

The objective of mailings, networking and most other marketing and promotional activities is to persuade potential users of your services to meet you and discuss what you have to offer. Only when you are face to face with the person who will buy your services can you begin to sell.

When meeting a potential client for the first time, the following points apply:

- Do not be in a hurry to start offering specific services. Get the person talking, and listen carefully to what is said. Only when you know exactly what is needed can you begin to put forward ideas. This way you are not selling a product, you are solving a problem for which the potential client is already seeking a solution.
- Do not rush into detail. Unless the required solution is very simple, you will need to spend time carrying out research before making a proposal. A sensible client will understand this, but they usually want some early indication of cost. Without knowing in detail what the assignment will involve, giving an accurate cost estimate is going to be difficult, so restrict yourself to quoting day rates and the price of more easily measured services like surveys, needs assessments and standard training programmes.

> *The client will usually be satisfied if convinced that you can:*
>
> – demonstrate a fair and systematic approach to costing
> – offer rates that are within an acceptable range
> – agree to prepare a proposal that offers alternative strategies in cost-sensitive areas
> – promise a price that relates exactly to the proposal content with no hidden extras.

- When a proposal is requested, be sure to negotiate sufficient time to do it well – *and then go about preparing it along the lines we discussed on Tuesday and Wednesday.*

> If, as is usually the case, other consultants are bidding for the same assignment, you will be chosen not because of the quality of your work, since the potential client has no way of measuring that, but on the quality of your proposal.

Newsletters

Once a consultancy becomes established, a useful way of keeping actual and potential clients informed about your services is to publish a regular newsletter. Every six months is the most common frequency for newsletters but some very active consulting firms produce four or more issues a year. The stated purpose of a newsletter is to tell people what the consultancy has been doing. The thinly veiled secondary purpose is to remind clients of the services they may already have used, in the hope they will

use them again, and to arouse interest in any new services
you have developed.

Newsletter contents

In addition to reminders about existing services and details
of new ones, a newsletter might contain:

- information about new clients (always get the client's
  permission before publishing)
- news items – any media cover the consultancy has
  received, conferences, presentations and other public
  appearances, involvement in research etc.
- short articles on subjects relevant to the consultancy's
  services
- extracts from articles, reports and surveys that will
  interest clients (get written permission from copyright
  holders before using any published material)

Designing and producing a newsletter

Start the newsletter with a leader commenting on topical
issues and highlighting any new developments in
legislation, economic trends etc. that will affect clients in
areas where your services could be of help.

Producing a regular newsletter is demanding of time and
requires special skills which some consultants will have to
acquire, but the benefits to the business will almost
certainly make this effort worthwhile. Thanks to personal
computers and desktop publishing software, the task of
putting together an attractively presented newsletter is now
a simple matter and the cost is modest.

Growing the business

Once a consulting business is off the ground and trading well, it is only natural to want to see it grow and prosper; but take care not to get too enthusiastic about growth unless it is part of a well-thought-out plan.

Ideally, a small consultancy should be allowed to grow naturally and in direct response to client demand. Pushing too hard for growth can involve unnecessary risks.

These risks include:

- *financial* – forced growth will require the investment of time and money in marketing and promoting. If this strategy does not deliver the expected work, there could be serious financial consequences.
- *erratic demand* – aggressive business development can lead to surges and troughs in workload as areas of activity are rapidly opened up, only to die back when limited needs are satisfied. Coping with surges can overstretch resources and lead to poor performance. Troughs can create financial problems; especially for those tempted to buy in resources to help with the surges.

Small consultancies seem to grow best from the steady, natural development that comes from identifying with a market, establishing a reputation for quality and reliability and building up a network of common-interest clients.

Finding the right niche

Finding the right niche in the market has been the making of many small consultancies – and enabled several of them to become large consultancies.

A market niche can take several forms. It can be:

- *product-based* – based on a particular kind of training programme or service. There are several highly successful consulting businesses that offer just one specialised service.
- *sector-based* – many sectors like to have their needs satisfied by consultants with a special understanding of their area of activity. This policy often means that many consulting firms are excluded by organisations in these sectors, leaving a profitable niche for a generalist consultant who is perceived as having the necessary 'special understanding' of the sector.
- *based on some innovation or special technique* – there are obvious examples of this in computing and other technology applications, but there are just as many opportunities for innovation in management functions like operations, marketing and human resources.

Providing a quality service

Everything we have looked at today and yesterday is vital to the survival and growth of an emerging consultancy. Marketing, promoting and the hard grind of getting services known to potential clients, are tasks that must be done, and done well. But all this energy and enthusiasm will be lost if the quality of what a consultant has to offer, and the skill with which it is provided, are below the high standards most clients demand.

Consultants are frequently called in because a client needs something that they cannot supply for themselves. More often than not, this 'something' is knowledge and experience; and many would-be consultants believe that having that knowledge and experience is all they need to be successful. It is not. To be successful, a consultant must be equally skilled in the art of delivering service.

If you keep in mind these contrasting demands, *to display excellence in what you have to offer your clients and also in the way you deliver it*, you will be a success.